HOW TO TAKE CARE OF OLD PEOPLE WITHOUT GETTING WORKED UP: A Beginner's Guide To Family Caregiving

Fiona Brown

Table of Contents

Chapter 1: INTRODUCTION TO CAREGIVING

WHO EXACTLY IS A CAREGIVER?
Caregivers often provide emotional, physical, and psychological support to others, indicating that they work in the human services field. People in this sector care for someone with a handicap or a chronic condition, and the majority of the time, they work as senior carers. They may provide care at nursing facilities as well as in the client's home on a stay-in or periodic basis.

Aside from professional carers, a family member may also care for a loved one. Since 2015, the amount of family carers has climbed by 9.5 million. Unlike being a trained caregiver, caring for the ill or being an aged caregiver is done sincerely with no expectation of reward or monetary recompense.

Being a caretaker in a relationship (other than the patient's) might complicate matters, particularly if the patient requires the caregiver practically all of the time. If you choose to be a caretaker for someone, you must be prepared for the potential drawbacks of the job.

WHAT ROLE DO CAREGIVERS PLAY?

The tasks and obligations of a caregiver are determined by their connection and the level of assistance required by the patient. However, recall that you are there to care for, empower, and inspire that individual, not to descend into their lives and make decisions for them.

If a family member is now an elder caretaker, they should usually perform the following:

- Assist the patient with washing, grooming, clothing, exercising, and transferring into and out of the wheelchair, automobile, and toilet.
- Buy groceries, cook meals, conduct housework, washing, and do other errands for the elderly.
- Provide standard health care services such as medication administration and prescriptions, appointments, and medication reminders.
- Constant company, emotional support, and monitoring are provided.
- Create a care plan, keep track of the patient's health, and communicate any changes or findings to and from the doctor.
- Evaluate their own needs, the needs of the persons they are caring for, and the other relatives concerned.
- Allow care recipients to make their own decisions and alternatives, rather than imposing an ultimatum.

- Allow the patient to make their own decisions and accept responsibility for their actions.

These are the sorts of caregivers you may learn about when it comes to elder care.

1. Private-duty caregivers

These individuals are contracted via an agency. These caregivers are normally vetted, bonded, and insured by the agency. Families may get a backup caregiver via a caregiver agency if their booked caregiver is unable to work a shift.

2. Independent caregivers

Also known as private carers, these individuals should not be confused with private-duty caregivers. Independent carers are now employed by an agency. While the cost may be lower, families that pay for these carers assume the risk of having someone in their house.

3. Family caregiver

They are family members who volunteer to care for a loved one. Children, spouses, and other family members may serve as caretakers. They may perform other employment in addition to their obligations and are typically not compensated for their efforts.

4. Respite caregiver

This is someone who provides care for a short amount of time to allow a family caregiver a rest. These carers may be on private duty or autonomous, but the function suggests that they are not long-term caretakers.

ADVANTAGES OF HAVING A CAREGIVER

Caregivers bring several advantages to elders and their families. Here are some of the advantages:

1. In-home caregivers provide seniors with the freedom they need to age in place. Caregivers may assist elders with washing, cooking, medicine reminders, homecare, and other tasks, allowing them to stay at home and maintain their daily routine. Many elders may not want to relocate to a facility, and a caretaker allows them to do so.

2. Peace of mind: Many family members may be concerned about their loved ones, particularly if they reside far away. A caregiver can offer the peace of mind that family members and elders deserve. Caregivers may accompany elders to keep them safe and healthy. It might be a tremendous comfort to have a caregiver you can trust with your loved one.

3. Cost: Hiring a caregiver on a 24-hour basis is sometimes less expensive than

relocating into a facility. Seniors may also engage caregivers for particular hours, ensuring that they get care just when they need it rather than paying for hours of care that they may not require. Your insurance coverage may cover in-home care, decreasing the cost even more.

*****

People who care for family members of origin are referred to as "family caregivers," while those who tend for their family of preference are also referred to as "family caregivers." Members of their church, neighbors, or close acquaintances might be among them. Family caregivers play an important role in health care since they are often the primary source of vital patient information.

Consider health care as a three-legged chair to grasp the significance of a caregiver. One leg of the stool is occupied by family caregivers; another by healthcare practitioners (doctors, nurses, etc.); and the third by the care receiver. Health care cannot be as successful as it needs to be without all three legs.

Chapter 2: TIPS FOR A FIRST-TIME CAREGIVER

Being a caretaker, whether gradually or unexpectedly, may be stressful and exhausting, particularly if you're also working and/or raising a family. There will be a lot of trial-and-error learning as you traverse this new world of aiding with everyday chores since no one will teach you what to do or what is required of you.

Welcome to the club of carers. It might be an anxious and unsure environment, but we've laid down some guidelines to help you get started on the right foot. Here are some measures that new carers should be mindful of.

1. Examine the circumstances.
It's critical to speak with the care recipient, as well as their relatives and friends to get a sense of what you're getting into and what

you'll be dealing with daily. This will provide a baseline for what has been going on, how long it has been going on, and what type of treatment will be necessary. From health to economics, it is critical to listen to and regard the care recipient's opinions, beliefs, and aspirations.

Obtain a thorough medical evaluation of the care recipient's overall health from their physicians to detect any underlying concerns, identify dangers, and discuss treatment choices. In addition, a careful assessment will help determine the level and types of care needed. Some hospitals, Area Agencies on Aging, municipal or county organizations, Caregiver Resource Centers, or other state or corporate groups provide free or low-cost consulting and evaluations for older individuals.

2. Inform yourself.

Power comes from knowledge. Perform research on the course of any sickness or impairment that the care-recipient has been identified with, as well as their medicines and any medical procedures. Investigate your options online, study books and brochures, and speak with specialists and others in similar circumstances. Save essential information for future reference.

Obtaining knowledge and training can assist you in feeling competent about the many activities you conduct. Learn first aid, stroke indications, and symptoms, as well as particular instruction in the use of assistive devices and dealing with problematic behavior.

3. Resources for research.

Caregivers have access to a number of information. Community groups, such as your local Agency on Aging (AAA), may give useful information, recommend services such as food delivery, transportation, or home maintenance, and point you in the direction of area assisted living facilities and/or daycare programs.

4. Make a care plan.

Make a list of your immediate and long-term requirements to create a care plan. Some caring activities are time-consuming, while others are challenging. Determine what chores the person getting care can still complete on their own and which will need help.

Buying groceries, making meals, cleaning, doing dry cleaning, driving, assisting with personal hygiene and/or dressing, dealing with physicians, paying bills/handling financial and other legal problems, and other duties are common. Determine what you are capable and willing to perform and, where feasible, outsource the rest. Remember that this plan is flexible and will alter as the care receiver's requirements change.

5. Delegate

Rally the troops after you've identified what you need assistance with. Determine who can help with what and when among community services, pals, family, and neighbors. For jobs such as lawn maintenance, you may need to consider hiring a professional. Make a list of everyone you've recruited, along with their contact information. An email list or online scheduling applications may aid in the coordination and tracking of appointments and work allocations.

6. Make a secure living space.

Make the care receiver's surroundings as safe as possible. This may include making changes to the house to fit their requirements, such as placing grab bars in the bathroom to aid with balance or making the home handicapped-friendly.

7. Take good care of yourself.
Who looks after the caregiver? That is also your responsibility. Caregivers are vulnerable to feelings of loneliness, stress, loneliness, burnout, and poor health. Caregivers are more prone than non-caregivers to suffer from depression, heart disease, high blood pressure, and other chronic diseases, as well as mortality.

It's tempting to put your own needs last, but remember to "fill your cup," as they say. Make time for yourself, exercise regularly, and don't neglect your routine checks. Self-care does not have to include a spa weekend; it may be as simple as being nourished and rested.

8. Seek assistance.
Connect with people who are in similar circumstances, either online or in person. Support groups may provide social and emotional support, practical information and guidance, and a secure and private

environment to vent concerns, exchange ideas, and learn new caring practices. Furthermore, support programs and services such as counseling, respite, and house adaptations may be provided by local government agencies, faith-based groups, or workplace initiatives.

THINGS TO PUT IN PLACE

1. Organize important documents. Start having such chats while someone is in relatively good health. Begin by asking yourself, "What would happen if any of us had an accident?" If the caregiver can look in the mirror, they will be able to say, 'These are the things we all should have in place.' Try not to focus only on the elderly person, since none of us appears to know. And be aware that you will need to revisit that discussion. You may not always attain the desired result the first time around.

Complete the papers as soon as possible.
Perhaps the most valuable present you can
give your household is a binder of legal
documentation that will ensure everyone is
prepared in the event of an emergency.
You'll need two forms to get started. "How is
it kept?" Many of the paperwork you'll need
differ by state and may need the presence of
witnesses and potentially a notary. They all
need some thinking about how you wish to
be tended to during an ailment or at the end
of life.

Remember to keep your online account
credentials safe. Finding passwords and
accounts is a huge difficulty for one in every
three carers. Approximately half of the
carers report they lack legal authority or
passwords to access internet accounts such
as utility accounts, financial institutions,
credit cards, and social media sites.

2. Organize medical records.

Experienced caregivers advise making a binder for clinical records that you may take with you to doctor's visits. Keep track of different health providers, insurance details and payments, prescriptions, and notes about key health events and patient issues.

However, if a binder is too traditional for you, digital organizing may be a better solution. There are many applications available to assist carers to keep organized.

- Online Organizers: You may construct a digital binder of financial and health records using online services such as Google Drive or Dropbox. You may make separate files for each member of your family.

- Carezone is a basic app that lets you scan medicines, create reminders, manage appointments, and order refills all in one spot.

- Team Apps: CaringBridge and Caring Village link you with groups of individuals to organize the care of a loved one. Users of CaringBridge establish a personal blog to share health updates, images, and other information with a group of friends or relatives. Caregiving may be coordinated by a smaller, established group of individuals using Caring Village. Schedules, prescription lists, essential papers, and a private group chat option are all included.

- Monitoring: Amazon's Alexa gadget now includes Care Hub, which allows individuals to watch the activities of an elder or other person in their custody, set medicine reminders, and "drop in" via video.

3. Examine the house for security and caregiving.

Most individuals become caretakers to keep their loved ones in their own or a family member's home, or because they cannot afford an old people's home. However, it may become evident that changes are required over time. Stair and bath railings, higher toilet seats, and greater lighting may be required, as may the removal of area rugs or debris that might cause falls.

4. Prepare for change.

While your objective may be to retain your loved one at home, you should still look at choices for assisted living or senior facility care. Many of these clinics have waiting lists, so begin your investigation as soon as possible.

Chapter 3: DUTIES AND RESPONSIBILITIES OF A CAREGIVER

The basic responsibilities of a caregiver:

- Personal care assistance includes washing and grooming, clothing, toileting, and exercise.
- Basic food preparation includes meal preparation, grocery shopping, cleaning, laundry, and other tasks.
- General health care includes monitoring medication and prescription consumption, appointment reminders, and drug administration.
- Mobility aid includes assistance with getting into and out of a pushchair, automobile, or shower.
- Personal supervision entails offering regular company as well as general oversight.

- Transportation includes transportation to and from events, conducting errands, and assistance getting into and out of a wheelchair-accessible vehicle.
- Emotional assistance entails being a consistent companion and support in all situations. personal, medical, and emotional
- Caring for the elderly includes orienting or stabilizing someone suffering from Alzheimer's disease or dementia, as well as transmitting information from a physician to family members.
- Back-up care (or respite) services: offering a break for other carers.
- Home organization: assistance with arranging, packing, and cleaning for a vacation, as well as routine home maintenance and cleaning.
- Health monitoring entails adhering to a care plan and observing any changes in the individual's health, as well as

documenting and reporting any deviations.

WHAT TO EXPECT FROM A CAREGIVER

1. **Determine medical requirements**

Checking on the health of your elderly one is an important caregiver duty. You may be required to assist in the management of drugs and chronic diseases, as well as the assessment of pain levels. It's a good idea to have frequent conversations about your loved one's health with their doctor and other health experts.

2. **Make a care plan**.

While an in-home care provider cannot do exams or extensive medical procedures, they are certified to offer continuous monitoring and basic care. They may adhere to a care plan and keep an eye on the patient to make certain that no changes occur.

When you begin your caring journey, creating a care plan that meets your senior loved one's care requirements and objectives might be beneficial. A plan may assist you in determining how many hours of care your loved one will need each day and if you will require extra assistance to guarantee his or her health and safety.

If a problem arises, it is the caregiver's responsibility to confer with medical specialists to determine the best course of action.

3. Assist with necessities.

It is not unusual for older patients to battle with daily duties. Simple tasks like getting dressed, showering, and brushing teeth may become laborious as we age. They may even be severe in certain circumstances.

As a result, many of our elderly loved ones ignore their hygiene since it is hard to catch up with their regular activities. One caregiver's role is to help the patient with as much or as little as is required to keep up with their grooming regimen.

Grooming, using the restroom, and exercising are all much simpler with the assistance of a trained caregiver. A caregiver must offer help while enabling patients to maintain as much independence as possible. The bond between a caregiver and a patient is strengthened by establishing a cautious balance.

Check-in frequently and pay attention to particular signs and changes to ascertain if your loved one requires additional assistance.

4. Offer companionship.

Loneliness and despair are prevalent difficulties that contribute to a worse quality of life in seniors. While family gatherings and social events are common, many seniors feel lonely in between engagements.

A caregiver is more than simply someone who helps with non-medical activities regularly. They provide a consistent and dependable company. Another caregiver's job is to oversee patients and provide them with someone to chat with regularly. Caring for an elderly loved one provides an opportunity to improve your link and connection.

Care providers may even offer suggestions for new interests or ways to make new acquaintances. This kind of emotional support system enables each senior to continue to enjoy their social life. It provides the steadiness they need to flourish in their senior years.

5. Help with housework.

Maintaining a house might become more challenging as your loved one ages. Older folks may need assistance with dishwashing, trash disposal, and vacuuming. Even with your assistance, yard work, snow shoveling, and everyday upkeep may be too much for your loved one to undertake if they reside in a home. Consider if the convenience and assistance of a senior living community might benefit your loved one.

6. Keep track of prescriptions. Seniors, on average, take five prescriptions every day. Depending on individual requirements and diagnoses, that number might increase or decrease.

While the number of prescriptions taken is significant, it is believed that 75% of seniors do not take their tablets correctly. Some people may be taking medications that interfere with one another, while others may lack the mental ability to recall whether or not they've taken certain meds. You may assist your loved one to avoid overmedicating by setting up reminders and monitoring his or her meds.

A skilled caregiver collaborates closely with medical specialists to ensure that their patients take their medications correctly. They assist lower the likelihood of major difficulties associated with inappropriate medicine usage by providing tablets and correctly educating each of their patients.

7. Review your care plan frequently.

The plan of care will need to be changed as the circumstances around you and your loved one change. It should be reviewed regularly to evaluate what is working, what isn't, and what needs to be changed. Maintain regular touch with your loved one's doctor and other healthcare providers to address any changes.

8. Make food.

With aging, food preparation might become more challenging. Your loved one may lose the motivation or ambition to cook if they live alone. Cooking might be dangerous in certain situations due to memory and balance concerns. As a caregiver, you may assist your loved one with food shopping, meal preparation, or finding alternatives to guarantee sufficient nourishment.

Many individuals struggle to get their necessary nutrition due to dietary constraints, preferences, and demands. It might be even more difficult for folks who are unwell or elderly to prepare healthful and enjoyable meals. Allow a carer to assist you.

Caregivers are educated to manage any interactions that certain meals may have with drugs, as well as to prevent allergies. Creating extremely healthy meal planning is simply one of several caregiver tasks, in addition to interactions.

They will engage the assistance of their people to make sure that each dish is suited to their dietary requirements and personal preferences while being tasty and healthy. Aside from menu planning, most carers will also undertake the essential grocery shopping and meal preparation to make mealtime simpler than before.

9. Assist with mobility and transfer.

Falls pose a significant risk to the health of old people. Your loved one may have trouble moving or relocating — for example, from their bed every morning to an armchair in the afternoon. You may take efforts as a caregiver to assist avoid falls and keep your loved one safe and comfortable.

10.   Make transportation available.

Transportation is a major issue for the elderly. Most seniors outlive their capacity to drive safely by 7 to 10 years, yet many continue to drive often, endangering themselves and others.

Public transit and driving may no longer be safe alternatives as your loved one matures. To get your loved one to doctor's appointments and other activities, you may need to check into senior transportation options.

Transportation to and from activities, as well as assisting patients in and out of wheelchairs, is one potential caregiver role. This alleviates the stress and worries that older persons and their loved ones may experience while planning transportation.

11.   Family Assistance

It might be tough for a family member to accept the indications of aging that their elders may exhibit. Many people are unsure how to assist or deal with the situation. A caregiver is available to assist both the patient and the family. They provide knowledge, ideas, and strategies to help families. Family members may maintain their independence while providing the attention that their loved ones need with the assistance of an in-home caregiver.

SKILLS EXPECTED OF A CAREGIVER

Given all of these obligations, it's reasonable to conclude that carers put a lot of effort into the lives of their patients. These essential talents and characteristics are part of what distinguishes an extraordinary and effective caregiver for your beloved one.

1. Compassion

Compassion is among the most important qualities of a caregiver, particularly if they are assisting someone with physical or mental problems. Caregivers must take the time to learn about their patients' struggles to empathize with them.

Even basic things like keeping eye contact, speaking directly to their patients, and guiding them through an uncomfortable circumstance may produce good improvements in your family member's viewpoint and experience. Caregivers may assist their clients to cope with the everyday physical, mental, and emotional sadnesses of life by displaying compassion and understanding for their needs.

2. Flexibility

Patients with disabilities may not follow a typical weekly routine, thus carers must be fully aware that each day with their service users may be highly variable depending on pain levels and emotional condition.

Caregivers must be ready to be flexible with their patients' feelings, as well as to be accessible outside of normal work hours for additional care or in the event of an emergency.

3. Commitment to long-term care
Caregiver-patient relationships evolve with time and trust, so creating a solid one will take time. Caregivers who can devote themselves to their patient's care on a long-term level have a higher chance of developing a good connection, which leads to increased dependability and trust.

Too much turnover may make the patient cautious about getting to know caregivers, straining communication in new interactions.

4. Communication skills that work

Being a caregiver requires excellent communication skills. Many clients need medicine reminders, companionship, and aid with daily living tasks, and they rely on day-to-day talks to comprehend their care plan. Caregivers may provide quality treatment and alter their approach depending on feedback from their customers if they communicate with them on a regular and continuous basis. Clients may feel abandoned and unclear of where the connection stands if a caregiver is unable to communicate properly.

5. Patience and problem-solving abilities

The fact is that not everyone is capable of becoming a full-time caregiver since it demands a great deal of patience and understanding for individuals with special needs.

It is not simple to care for persons with
disabilities, therefore all caregivers must
have a patient attitude, knowing that they
can always depend on their problem-solving
talents to find a way out of any difficulty.

Caregivers must be able to recalibrate
themselves when confronted with changes
or obstacles during the day. On a personal
level, they must recognize that their patients
are individuals with a broad variety of
emotions and mobility challenges. A good
caregiver will take the time to understand
their patients and work with them through
every difficulty and challenge.

Chapter 4: STEPS TO TAKE WHEN AN ELDERLY ONE NEEDS HELP

Some elderly parents appear more withdrawn. Others begin making charges against others, stating that someone has taken or moved something, or becoming paranoid.

These developments raise several concerns for many adult children. What's the problem? What is going on? It's a transition that no one wants to make and one most people are unprepared for: the day when you may have to start supporting your elderly parent.

And for many, there's an additional challenge: most elderly parents don't want much support from their grown children. They may perceive it as an intrusion or violation of privacy.

Some parents may even refuse to acknowledge that they are experiencing problems, despite situations that seem evident — and alarming — to you.

By the time you notice changes and have security concerns, it's highly feasible that you're correct: your parent does need some kind of assistance. So, how should you become engaged, particularly if previous efforts have been unsuccessful?

It's not going to be easy. These scenarios are problematic from a medical and eldercare standpoint, and they tend to elicit painful feelings in both elderly parents and adult children. It's not going to be easy. But it may be made simpler if you discover the best methods to do it—as well as what to avoid doing.

Here's a rundown of the steps:

- Collect facts about the issue by looking for particular signals that an aging parent needs assistance or is in danger, and by politely obtaining information from others.

- Before you make any further efforts to persuade your parents to make changes, acquire their viewpoint so you can grasp how they perceive the problem and what is essential to them. (During these early chats, don't even think about trying to convince them to comprehend, agree, or accept what's going on.)

- Learn what an appropriate health and eldercare intervention looks like to direct plans if there are indicators of memory loss, safety concerns, or losses in independence.

- Learn some legal basics concerning indicators of mental "incompetence" or "incapacity," as well as legal instruments, that may help you better support your aging parent.

- Create an actionable strategy that tackles the most significant issues, based on what you've learned so far about your parents' circumstances and goals.

- Connect with your parent and persuade them to agree to at least some adjustments. Put your strategy into action. Be ready to make multiple efforts, since this is frequently required.

STEPS IN THE DEVELOPMENT OF A CARE PLAN

1. **Assess the magnitude of the issue.**

The first step is to determine how badly your loved one requires assistance. Spend some time inspecting the home for any safety hazards, and consider how your loved one travels about the house daily. This can allow you to identify how quickly you need to act. For example, if a senior is immobile and is released from the hospital, you must make preparations for help before he or she arrives home.

Seniors who need 24-hour care may depend on experienced live-in caregivers to provide healthy meals and snacks, aid with personal hygiene activities such as washing and grooming, and offer prescription reminders on time.

2. Discuss your loved one's problems with them.

Seniors who are active in making choices regarding their care are more inclined to follow the plans of their relatives. Inquire about the forms of assistance your loved one believes he or she needs. Take notice if your loved one expresses dread of going about everyday activities. Your loved one should also be able to do the majority of the tasks without getting weary or in too much discomfort. If your loved one expresses uneasiness or fears of being wounded, these are the places where you should focus care.

3. Put up a proper priority list.

After speaking with your loved one, you may wish to chat with others who may assist you in identifying his or her needs. Doctors, relatives, and neighbors are all great places to start. Gather information on what these folks say, and be sure to incorporate some of your own opinions. Remember that most elders will ultimately need assistance with personal hygiene, cleaning, and daily food preparation. You should also consider social and emotional requirements.

There are several reasons why elders may need home care. Some people with Alzheimer's disease may need daily mental stimulation, whilst others may merely require part-time support with exercise and basic domestic duties.

4. Form a group to tackle each need.

Examine your list carefully and note down some names of persons you believe can assist you with each assignment. Remember that you don't want anybody to be overburdened with your loved one's care. Professional caregivers are critical members of this team. They will not only be able to offer others a rest, but they are also well trained in elder care.

5. Make independence your number one priority.

Your loved one should get all the necessary help to feel secure at home. You don't want to make the error of removing your parent's ability to care for his or her overall health. Promoting senior independence entails providing just enough assistance to protect them from harm while also encouraging them to undertake things on their own.

6. Implement the strategy.
Once you've devised a strategy, you must move rapidly to put this into effect. This allows you to assist your loved one before he or she suffers an accident or other health problem. You'll also be able to observe how well your strategy is working. Be open to updating the plan as required, and keep in mind that planning a senior's care often necessitates making modifications over time.

Many older persons want to age in place, and others need assistance to keep living at home securely and pleasantly.

HOW TO ASSIST AGING PARENTS WITHOUT BEING TOO OBLIGATORY

Following a few basic guidelines may make a huge impact on how you give care. Above

all, remember to be mindful of your
behavior, words, and tone, and how these
influence your aging parents. Self-awareness
is essential for keeping even the finest
intentions in check, changing your approach
as needed, and trying to make amends when
you fall beyond your parents' bounds.

1. **Allow aging parents to lead.**

If it's possible, work with your parents, not
for them. . While this method may take
longer than doing things yourself, it allows
Mom and Dad to keep some of their
freedom by allowing them to take the lead.
This may improve your parents' self-esteem
and maintain their functioning skills.

Some elders refuse to participate in daily
duties, expecting their family carers to do
so. This not only places a huge lot of burden
on caretakers but also often sets seniors up
for a rapid decrease in physical and mental
functioning. Your objective should be to

increase their independence rather than to increase their reliance on you.

2. Allow parents to control when and how you help.

Allow your parents to come to you rather than swooping in to finish every unfinished job or address every difficulty. When they show you what components of a certain task they need your aid with, try to restrict your support to just those areas for the time being.

Sometimes parents find it difficult to seek help directly. Pay close attention when Mom or Dad discusses their stories and opinions with you. If they express concerns or frustrations about a specific chore, inquire whether they may benefit from your assistance. Perhaps if they do not comply, you will have shown that you care about their well-being and are eager to assist them. Many elderly people value just knowing that someone values and listens to them. Feel free to extend the offer as many times as necessary, but don't press the matter unless their safety or survival is in jeopardy.

If your mother or father does not have reasonable goals of what they can achieve for themselves, you need to find a gentle method to assist them to understand your point of view. Communicating your real care for their well-being is often the most effective method to make your argument. If they refuse your assistance, inquire as to who they would take assistance from. Seniors may be more tolerant of outside assistance from professional carers hired via a home care agency. In this manner, parents may seek the help they need without jeopardizing their ties with their children. Whatever the answer is, make sure you all work together to solve the issue.

3. Show respect.

Before you plunge in, be sure you have permission. For example, if you accompany your elderly one to a doctor's visit, don't assume they want you to accompany them inside the examination room. Instead, ask whether they want you to stay the whole time or if you should simply come in at the end to make sure YOUR issues are discussed.

Remember that regardless of how old they are or how their skills change, your parents are always your parents. They are entitled to be treated with decency and respect. As difficult as caring for elderly parents might be, try to avoid being harsh or disrespectful. While many people refer to tending to an aging parent as a "role reversal," it's crucial to remember that older adults are not children who want parental guidance. Aging is challenging, and most elders do not want it to be difficult. Remember that the more you persist in managing a problem, the more probable Mom and Dad are to refuse your "assistance."

4. Install safety nets.

Irrespective of whether or not your aging parents want or accept your assistance, do your best to put up a support system that will keep them safe while interfering as little as possible with their daily routine. An excellent example is a medical alert system. Wearable pendants are inconspicuous and give peace of mind to you and your parents in the case of a medical emergency or an accident, such as a fall.

Senior care goods might also assist your aging parents to maintain their freedom. Investigate assistive equipment, such as medication dispensers and mobility aids, that may help them with activities of daily living (ADLs).

An occupational therapist may assist you and your parents in investigating all alternatives for assisting them in living as independently and securely as possible. If your parents have the necessary tools, they can tend to their requirements with little assistance. Accepting new ways of doing things might be tough for seniors, but many are willing to adapt if it means they won't have to rely on others for help.

5. Put their well-being first.
If your elderly one is acting carelessly, ignoring themselves, or threatening their safety, intervening is in their best interests, and you may need to be much more firm. This situation is common when a parent is suffering from cognitive difficulties. Seniors with Alzheimer's disease or other kinds of dementia may be unaware that their skills have altered and may continue to follow their typical habits even though it is unsafe. Loss of memory and poor judgment may make even the most routine everyday actions perilous. It is your responsibility at

that time to interfere notwithstanding their
complaints.

Distinguish between protection and
everything else. When your parent's safety is
at stake, you may need to take action by
gently taking over. This isn't about your
desire for things to be done in a particular
manner or at a specific time. Let go of what
isn't important and concentrate on the goal:
making your parents safe, healthy, and
happy.

Chapter 5: ACTIVITIES FOR ELDERLY PEOPLE

What hobbies do seniors enjoy? As a family caregiver or highly qualified caregiver, you may find yourself repeating regular routines with individuals in your care. Schedules are necessary for people you care for, but they may also become monotonous, making you and the one you care for less enthused about your moments together. Many elders lose the capacity to participate in activities they previously enjoyed, but caregivers have a rare chance to be innovative and assist seniors in resuming those lost interests.

Take note:

1. Make inquiries.

Choose to know them and inquire about their interests. Take the time to go deeper and see if there is anything they were doing

that you could modify so that they can do it
again.

2. Be innovative.

Consider other activities for the elderly in
your care if they are unable to engage in one.
For example, if they like fishing, recommend
that they volunteer to teach a fly tying
lesson.

3. Consider their capabilities.

There might be physical and mental limits
that make some activities difficult for you.
Keep these limitations in mind and
concentrate on activities that they can
accomplish easily.

There are several activities available to
elders. It may need some thought and
preparation on your side as the caregiver,
but the aim is to keep your client satisfied.

ACTIVITIES SENIORS COULD PARTICIPATE IN

1. Invest time in reading.

Reading is an excellent hobby for senior people. It's a pleasant way to pass the time and keep the mind occupied. It may also help with memory, stress reduction, sleep, and delaying cognitive deterioration.

Whether your senior citizen prefers to read tangible books, periodicals, e-readers, or audiobooks, they may bury themselves in a well-told tale, gaze at images, or learn about a fascinating new subject. Another method for seniors to love reading and mingling is to form a book club with their pals.

2. Take up a range of interests.

Hobbies are ideal for elderly people who have restricted mobility.

Cooking, baking, birding, knitting, crochet, indoor or compartment gardening, using a musical instrument, or acquiring a foreign language are examples of low-movement activities.

This is also an excellent chance to learn anything new if they haven't had the opportunity to do so before. Learning is also an excellent technique to keep your mind engaged and avoid boredom.

3. Regular exercise

Even if your elderly relative is not ambulatory, there may still be activities they may take to keep their body moving.

They may obtain health and mood advantages whether they're sitting or standing, particularly with seated workouts like chair yoga routines. Other workout regimens may be done with or without a walker to decrease edema in the feet and ankles.

4. Be inventive.

Another enjoyable method for seniors to invest their time is to explore their artistic side.

Drawing, doodling, painting, and sculpting are all excellent methods to express oneself creatively. Making scrapbooks, arranging picture albums, or coming up with a family recipe book is all fun to do.

Additionally, being creative has health advantages. According to research, creative hobbies may assist individuals suffering from chronic illnesses, reduce negative emotions and boost good ones, release tension, and improve medical results.

5. Spend time outside.

Getting outdoors to spend some time in the surroundings is both calming and uplifting.

Even if your elderly relative can only walk to the porch or sit beside a large window due to their restricted movement, getting some cool breeze or observing the environment is a terrific daily exercise.

6. Have a good time with joyful guests.

Another excellent technique to occupy an older adult is to invite relatives or friends with infants or friendly dogs to pay a visit. Almost everyone gets excited when they see small children. Another guaranteed technique to provide joy and alleviate stress is to play with dogs.

7. Have fun with games.

Games and puzzles are excellent sources of entertainment. There are several options, and most of them may be enjoyed in groups with guests, one-on-one for bonding time together, or alone. Play some vintage games or card games, or do some jigsaw puzzles or crossword puzzles.

8. Take in some movies, TV programs, or music.

While watching television all day, every day is not a healthy activity, a movie or a few TV episodes may be a fun way to spend the day or week.

Watching TV might even cross with a passion. For example, an elderly relative could be interested in seeing a documentary on a subject they're studying.

Another enjoyable pastime is listening to (or singing along to) music. Music can alleviate tension, anxiety, and discomfort. It also boosts immunological function, enhances sleep, and aids memory.

9. Volunteer for charity causes.

Even if your elderly relative is unable to leave the house or is housebound, they may still contribute to society. This is a good approach to keeping involved and experiencing a feeling of purpose and success.

Contact local organizations, healthcare facilities, or religious groups to see if they have any tasks that your elderly relative may help with. This might include knitting or crocheting quilts or caps, making no-sew blankets, or assisting with the assembly of care packages.

10.   Organize and redecorate.

When you're confined at home, staring at the same landscape day after day, it's easy to get bored. Fortunately, there is a simple solution. Cleaning and redecorating in the spring! If you don't like massive home tasks, even arranging a room or two might make a great impact. After all, fresh surroundings provide new insights.

11.   Make use of the internet.

With social distance at the forefront of society right now, an increasing number of businesses and people have decided to make their information accessible on the internet. Many of them are also free. Look online for Broadway performances, ballet productions, musicals, e-sports, educational courses, workout classes, museum visits, zoo excursions, and other activities to do at home. There's so much going on on the internet right now!

12.   Take a seat and talk.
We're constantly hurrying about trying to get things done that we forget to sit and converse with our friends and relatives. But what is more essential than spending time with our loved ones?

Get a cup of coffee, chocolate, water, or whatever you want, and settle down to talk. If you're alone at home, you can always accomplish this via phone conversations and video chats.

13.   Bask in the sun.

Usually, spend 15 minutes outside in the fresh air if you have a garden or porch. Meditate, ponder, look out the window, take a bite, make some phone conversations, and sketch. There are several activities you may perform in your backyard. Simply open a window if you don't have a yard. Breathing in the fresh air and feeling the sun on your body will keep you calm and joyful. Not to mention that it will help you sleep soundly.

14.   Experiment with fresh recipes.

Every day, we eat three meals, with beverages and snacks somewhere in. And when we eat too much, eating may become a tedious effort. But it doesn't have to be like that. Try some new dishes to liven things up. You may get new dinner ideas by searching on Pinterest and YouTube. Or make your own!

Also, don't forget to snap photos. Your relatives and friends will be delighted to see what you've created.

15.   Create your material.

While the rest of the world is at home, individuals all around the globe are hungry for internet material. If you've ever wanted to establish your own Youtube page, TikTok account, or podcast, here is the place to be. Alternatively, if you've ever wanted to write tales, provide advice, provide suggestions, or just tell your life experience, here is your chance! It's simple to get started, and you'll undoubtedly meet some new friends along the road.

Have fun and contribute to the world in ways that only you can.

Chapter 6: SHARING CARE WITH SIBLINGS

Partnering with siblings to care for elderly parents may be nearly as difficult for some families as the caring itself.

IMPROVING CAREGIVING AND SIBLING RELATIONSHIPS

1. **Concentrate on the level of your parent's attention.**

It's important to note that when siblings work together to tend to elderly parents, the parents get better care altogether. Furthermore, when siblings are at odds, parents are likely to be aware. It will most likely irritate them that they have unwittingly created a tough scenario.

Using time and energy arguing takes away from the time and energy you might be using to lobby for your older senior.

Consider these things to help you set aside disputes for the benefit of your parents.

2. Avoid being trapped in childhood roles.

When functioning together to care for elderly parents, it's natural to revert to childhood routines and rivalries. Siblings may strive to be the favorite or struggle for decision-making power.

It's a good idea to remind yourself that everyone is now a grownup and that you don't have to continue your childhood behavior patterns. Learn to approach each other with the same respect you would any other adult.

3. Eliminate sexist stereotypes.

Caregiving obligations should not be assigned based on gender preconceptions. Brothers should not expect their sisters to perform all of the labor since they are used to women handling care of the family.

Siblings can only work well together when gender prejudices are ignored.

Instead of splitting jobs based on gender, have an honest talk about the sorts of chores you believe are most suited to your and your siblings' abilities. If you believe their sibling unjustly expects you to perform particular tasks because of your gender, talk to them about the reasons you think this way and how they may be more active in sharing those obligations.

4. Keep open lines of contact with your siblings.

It will be simpler to divide responsibilities and discuss goals of how each of you wishes to share care if you have strong and coherent communication amongst siblings. If you need assistance with a specific area of care, discuss it with your sibling(s) rather than just assume they will be aware. Check in with each other frequently and share personal plans, such as travel, to ensure that someone is available to care for your parent's needs.

5. Don't strive for equality; instead, do what makes the greatest sense.

A fully fair division of caring duties is both unlikely and impractical. Instead, distributing duties in ways that are unique based on each person's particular position benefits the whole team.

Siblings will live at differing distances from their parents, in diverse financial conditions, and with varying life obligations. It's normal for one or two people to assume greater responsibility than others.

Inequality is not necessarily a negative thing. When one or two persons can react fast to events or are present in person more often, they may assume the lead. Of course, it is still necessary for all siblings to participate. Having frequent family gatherings to check in and recognize everyone's efforts keeps things on track.

6. Be nice to one another.

Caregiving is a difficult profession that puts everyone's patience to the test. And other parents are difficult, nasty, or show no thanks at all. When siblings are friendly to one another, it makes the work simpler. Furthermore, you may express your grievances to one another and get encouragement, knowing that you all comprehend.

7. Determine who will be the main caregiver.

Speak out if you are unable to be the primary caretaker due to your employment, family obligations, geography, or other factors. Allow someone else to take the initiative if they have the time and ability. It's difficult enough to be a caretaker without feeling like you're not the appropriate person for the job.

8. Discuss your strengths.

Determine who wants to do what once you've decided what your parents require assistance with. If you don't fully despise the work at hand, you're more likely to say yes when invited to assist. Even though you love your parents and would like to try to assist their aging in place, you won't be able to provide them with the care they demand if you have a bad attitude.

Talking about your abilities, interests, and shortcomings may assist guide the allocation of caregiving tasks in a manner that avoids traditional gender standards. For instance, if a sibling is good with money, let them handle the finances; if culinary is a strength, let them handle meal preparation. Naturally, there will be certain jobs that neither you nor your sibling(s) wish to complete. In these situations, it is critical to maintain open lines of communication to identify and solve the reason why no one wants to accomplish a certain assignment. This may assist you and your siblings in reaching an agreement that is agreeable to all parties concerned.

9. Make a schedule.

Only accessible after 2 p.m. on weekends? Write it down and discuss it with your siblings. Although this does not guarantee that you will not be requested to assist outside of that period, it does ensure that your family is aware of your availability. It will enable other family members to set relaxation periods for themselves. Should you decide that round-the-clock care is what your parents need, you should also identify areas where an organization's assistance may be required.

10. Collaboration is essential.

Working together to provide your parents with the greatest care possible will have a greater positive influence on their capacity to age in place. The less doubt everyone has about who is doing what and when, the simpler and smoother the switch to in-home care will be. And, if you ever discover yourself in need of a break because the mental and physical toll of becoming a family caregiver has been too much for you, call in reinforcements. Caregiver burnout is extremely real and may have a significant impact on one's mental health.

Long-distance caregivers may be a significant source of emotional support for the sibling who lives nearest to their parent. Calling your brother and paying attention may not seem to be much assistance, but a "listening ear" is frequently all they need. Caregivers who live a long distance away may also help with financial management, scheduling appointments, organizing services, and obtaining information on health services and drugs. Given the variety of delivery possibilities, online shopping for parents is also a terrific alternative.

Keep in mind that you are not alone. Having to care for a parent who has health issues is a path that a lot of us will face in our lifetimes. Conflicts are inevitable, and you and your family must understand how to resolve them.

11.   Recognize that conflicts might rise as parents age.

Seeing a parent deteriorate may be a difficult moment for all children concerned. This is regarded as anticipatory mourning. As the family begins this phase of transition, avoid laying blame on siblings who don't yet have a strong relationship with the elderly parent.

Many siblings are passing through a huge emotional upheaval around this time, which might bring up childhood memories. Seeing our parents age and finally die away is one of life's most difficult experiences, and everyone handles it differently. Male carers, for example, are often isolated, even though males currently account for around 45% of all family caregivers.

It is very natural to experience a variety of emotions when siblings band together to give care. You may have animosity against your estranged sibling from whom you have been alienated for many years. Alternatively, you may feel compelled to rival your sister being the more committed caretaker.

Because this is a trying time, try to be kind to yourself and your siblings. Recognize the fear, anguish, and stress that is prompting them to respond in this manner. This gentle approach will assist you in navigating impending challenges with tolerance and ease.

12. Recognize that your siblings may have varying opinions about what the parent requires.
Your ideas on what is useful and required for your aging parent may vary from those

of your siblings. It is normal for one kid to assume that the parent is at more risk than they are. Another youngster may ask if the same parent needs this much help at all.

Allow everyone an opportunity to reach an agreement when opposing viewpoints develop. Allow each sibling time to assimilate new information or assess the situation before making a decision. Make careful to share any information you get from a doctor, nurse, or geriatric specialist.

Also, take in mind that parents often teach different kids different things. So, if your sibling is informed that mom or dad is OK, they may have no option but to accept it. This is why everyone must understand both sides of the issue before making final judgments.

13. Never underestimate your siblings' responses.

It is all too easy to characterize your siblings as lazy, arrogant, greedy, or self-righteous. But keep in mind that they are likely just as terrified as you are. Each kid will have a unique connection with the aging parent, which will frequently influence how they approach caring responsibilities.

You will be able to speak with your siblings more honestly and successfully if you grasp this. Remember that they are not horrible children just because they do not behave or feel the same way you do.

Many caretakers would concede that caring for a loved one's needs may be a pleasant experience. However, it may also test your patience, causes ambivalence, and harms your mental well-being. You will be in a great spot to provide your parents with the loving care they need if you depend on your siblings for assistance.

Chapter 7: CAREGIVER STRESS

Caring for others is both gratifying and difficult. Being present when a loved one requires you is a key value for most carers and something you want to deliver.

However, a change in roles and reactions is often unavoidable. It's normal to feel furious, annoyed, fatigued, lonely, or depressed. Caregiver stress, which includes both mental and physical strain, is prevalent.

People who are caregiver stressed may be more vulnerable to fluctuations in their wellness. The following are possible causes of caregiver stress:

- Being a woman
- Having fewer formal years of schooling

- Living with the individual for whom you are caring Social isolation
- Suffering with depression
- Financial problems
- More hours spent caring for others
- Inability to solve difficulties and a lack of stress management
- Lack of choice in caring for others

SYMPTOMS OF CAREGIVER STRESS

As a caretaker, you may be so concentrated on your loved one that you don't know that your health and well-being are failing. Keep an eye out for the following indications of caregiver stress:

- Feeling overburdened or continually concerned
- Tired all the time
- Getting too much or too little sleep
- Putting on or losing weight
- Easily becoming upset or furious

- Loss of interest in previously enjoyed activities
- I'm depressed.
- Experiencing frequent headaches, body pain, or other physical issues
- Abuse of alcohol or drugs, especially prescribed pharmaceuticals

Too much stress, particularly over a long period, may be harmful to your health. As a caregiver, you are more prone to suffer from sadness or anxiety. Furthermore, you may not receive enough sleep, exercise, or eat a healthy diet, which raises your risk of medical issues including diabetes and cardiovascular disease.

DEALING WITH CAREGIVER STRESS

Even the most resilient individual may be tested by the emotional and physical responsibilities of caring. That is why it is important to use the various resources and products available to assist you in caring for your loved one. Remember that if you don't care for yourself, you won't be capable of caring for others.

To alleviate caregiver stress:

1. Accept assistance.

Prepare a list of methods that people can assist you, and then let the helper select what he or she wants to accomplish. A buddy, for example, may volunteer to accompany the person you manage for a stroll once or twice a week.

Concentrate on what you can provide. It's natural to feel guilty from time to time, but remember that no one is a "flawless" caretaker. Trust that you are doing your best and getting the right judgments possible at all times.

2. Set attainable objectives.
Divide complex activities into smaller stages
that can be completed one at a time. Make
lists and come up with a daily routine. Begin
to decline time-consuming requests, such as
organizing holiday feasts.

3. Make a connection.
Learn about caregiving services in your area.
Many communities arrange for
enlightenment on the illness your loved one
is suffering from. Transportation, food
delivery, and cleaning services may be
arranged.

4. Join a support network.
A support group may provide affirmation
and motivation, as well as problem-solving
skills in challenging circumstances. Support
groups are made up of people who
understand what you're going through. A
support group may also be a great way to
meet new people and form lasting
connections.

5. Seek social assistance.

Maintain contact with relatives and friends who can provide nonjudgmental emotional support. Make time each week to interact with others, even if it's only a stroll with a buddy.

6. Set personal health objectives.

Set objectives such as establishing a regular sleep schedule, finding time to be fit and active most days of the week, eating a nutritious diet, and drinking lots of water.

Many carers have trouble sleeping. A lack of quality sleep over an extended period might lead to health problems. Consult your doctor if you are having difficulty sleeping.

7. Consult your doctor.

Get the necessary vaccines and exams. Tell your doctor that you are a caregiver. Please express any problems or symptoms you may be experiencing.

WHAT TO DO WHEN CAREGIVER WORK BECOMES TOO MUCH

1. **Accept forgiveness and show appreciation.**

Caregivers' lives are fraught with the problems of evaluating care, communicating with others, and campaigning for care. Caregivers and recipients both have difficult days. Plans deviate, and appointments do not go as planned. Care recipients may not be feeling well, maybe in a poor mood, and may be verbally abusive to the caregiver and others inadvertently.

As the primary caregiver for an elderly parent or spouse, you are responsible for keeping things together. You are the one who can be relied on and who can solve problems. Caregivers learn via trial and error how to be efficient, stay calm, and manage life's activities.

Working carers arrange caregiving responsibilities before and after work hours, while evenings and weekends are spent caring for others. A hectic caring schedule may leave little time for spouses, kids, friends, and other activities. Caregiving strains family bonds. Even the most grade caregiver might be thrown off by caregiving hiccups. These are the occasions when caring for others becomes too much.

Taking a step back to pardon the event and the folks involved is the caregiver's first step in putting space between facts and the emotions of the incident. According to research, persons with strong self-control are more likely to forgive others and circumstances. Individuals who are diligent with their routines and activities have more personal and interpersonal success.

Expressing gratitude for even the tiniest item that goes well each day transforms negative thoughts into happy ones. Did you start the automobile this morning? Was your favorite song on the radio? Make it a daily practice to identify three things to be grateful for and to thank others.

2. Stop sacrificing yourself.

Caregivers prioritize the demands of an aged parent or partner who needs care above their own. Poor physical health is one of the first signs of caregiver martyr syndrome. Caregivers' health issues include headaches, stomach pains, difficulty sleeping at night, and sadness.

Instead of setting doctor's appointments for an aged parent or partner, the caregiver skips going to the doctor. "I'm not that ill," caregivers say, or "I've never been sick in my life." You have now become a carer. The rules have changed. Stop claiming that you are having health problems. Make and keep a doctor's appointment.

Do not quit attending Sunday services or meditating if you have a regular habit. Spiritual and mindful activities may help caregivers alleviate stress.

When was the last occasion you had a good time? Have you stopped making friends and socializing? Due to time restrictions, carers have or make time for themselves. When caring becomes too much, carers suffer from ill health and depression as a result of a lack of involvement in fun activities and socializing.

Increasing isolation leads to negative thoughts and loneliness. When caring becomes too much, locate a caregiver support network in person or on the phone to avoid being alienated from others. Sharing your emotions with someone who understands may be therapeutic.

3. Make time for yourself.

Physical and mental exercise are excellent ways for the brain to dispel anxiety and stress. On days when caring gets too much, take a stroll around your workplace or go for a walk outdoors. Start a walking club at your workplace at lunch. Join a gym and work out before work, at lunch, or on your way back from work.

Drive to the supermarket or the mall and go through the aisles. Drive to a playground, sit on a bench outdoors, and people-watch. Rock back and forth while sitting on a swing. Read a newspaper or a book that you like.

A change of environment, even if only for a short period, may shift sentiments of caregiving getting too much to feelings of caring being more bearable. Short pauses during the day are beneficial. Take up a hobby. Visit the library and check out publications that interest you. Consume

inspiring mags. Play some music. Find a
new activity to take with you, such as
crocheting, embroidery, or wood carving.

Activities that break up stressful mental
patterns are beneficial. Schedule and set
aside time for yourself. Make no more
excuses. A short 10-minute break might be
beneficial. Start your day 10 minutes sooner
by meditating. Begin with 10 minutes and
work your way up to three 10-minute
exercise breaks each day. Work your way up
from here. You've got this!

4. Discover new ways to make use of community resources.

Aging parents, partners, and other care
recipients experience feelings comparable to
caregivers who feel frustrated by caring.
Care recipients feel stuck since they must
take drugs and rely on adult close relatives
for care.

Caregivers benefit from having a schedule and a sense of purpose in their lives. They look forward to engaging and enjoyable activities. Negative behaviors and sadness emerge from feelings of loneliness and a lack of purpose in the absence of a pleasant daily routine. We all need a cause to get out of bed every morning and feel helpful.

Caregivers organize care and collaborate with medical experts and others to address health issues. These interactions provide an opportunity to inquire about community services for reducing days when caring becomes too much.

5. **Look for caregiver activities and diversions.**

Investigate opportunities for receiving assistance in caring for an elderly parent or spouse, such as activities and diversions. Are there any volunteers that could come and give the caregiver a pause? Can the caregiver enlist the help of friends or other relatives to help with care or activities? Is there a church or synagogue organization that visits elderly people in the community?

Can a parent or spouse participate in simple volunteer work? School-age children need mentors for reading. Senior centers have volunteer opportunities, outings, weekly lunches, and activities. Many senior centers offer transportation services.

When caregiving becomes too much, caregivers feel trapped. Options to investigate ways to use community resources might be the last thing on the mind of a caregiver when caregiving becomes too much.

6. Creating activities and diversions decreases isolation.

By talking to others in similar situations in a caregiving support group plus medical and other providers, you might come across the perfect idea to give you a regular break from caregiving responsibilities. By creating other ways for an aging parent or spouse to engage in life, you enrich their lives.

If an aging parent or spouse is homebound, books on tape, books or movies from the library, or other hobbies may offer an enjoyable activity. Being home all day with nothing to do but sit around the house, results in boredom and frustration for the care receiver. These behaviors transfer to interactions with the caregiver that are not positive. After a long day of work, visiting a negative or angry parent can be a dreaded experience.

Many caregivers fail to think that an aging parent or spouse might enjoy the company of others. Care receivers become as isolated and lonely as caregivers. Investigate community resources to minimize days when caregiving becomes too much.

7. Create pleasurable family activities that support socialization.

By creating regularly scheduled family activities, caregivers can reduce days when caregiving becomes too much. Caregiving becomes too much when all of the tasks and projects outweigh enjoyable activities.

The roles and responsibilities of caregiving are all-encompassing. As mentioned above, caregivers give up social activities and time with friends in favor of caregiving time. By creating a regular event at the home of an aging parent or spouse and inviting family and friends, creating regular opportunities for socialization is possible.

8. Give thought to scheduling a movie or television night.

Research funny and positive movies that everyone can enjoy. Humor is a positive response to stressful caregiving situations. Remember that your aging parent was once young and enjoys interacting like an equal rather than someone dependent on an adult child for help. If you are a spousal caregiver, think about the movies you enjoyed over the years with your spouse.

Seek out the top 10 lists of movies in different categories. Make movie night an event – and a celebration of fun. Schedule the night on the same day each month so that family and friends can add the event to their schedule and plan to attend. Make popcorn. Ask others who are attending to make and bring special treats. Rather than excluding an aging parent or spouse from gatherings, bring the gathering into the home.

NOTE THESE:

1. Let the patient lead.

Readers consistently talked about the importance of autonomy for the one receiving care. Include the person in care

decisions whenever possible. Make sure
doctors don't talk as if the patient isn't in the
room.

2. Focus on comfort.

Let comfort, joy, and pleasure be your
guideposts. Try not to nag. Readers talked
about the importance of small moments of
shared joy — listening to swing music or a
favorite crooner, playing card games, and
going for ice cream.

3. Listen to the experts.

Find experts to advise you, and listen to
them. Arm yourself with information from
caregiving organizations and support
groups. Trust your instincts. Ignore most of
the unsolicited advice you are likely to
receive.

4. Talk to other caregivers.

Support groups will be one of your best
resources.

5. Take care of yourself.

Even five- and 10-minute breaks during the day can help. Try keeping a gratitude journal, downloading a meditation app, or doing a six-minute workout to refresh your mind and body. Use adult day care or in-home caregivers from time to time so you can take a break. Take up friends on their offers to help, even if it's just to get your hair done. Exercising, sleeping, and eating well will make you a better caregiver for your loved one.

6. Shed the guilt.

Guilt is a common theme here, but experienced caregivers say it's important to know your limits, practice self-compassion, ask for help and remind yourself that the work you're doing is difficult and important.

THINGS TO DO WHILE TAKING A BREAK

1. Go on a fun trip.

Travel to an exotic island on a cruise, take a drive to see your favourite artist live, or organize a romantic weekend with your spouse. The goal is to have a good time while you're away from home. Try not to think about your elderly loved one while on vacation. It's OK to check in to see how he or she is coping, but don't make it your primary focus. A change of environment may help you rest and recover, giving you a unique outlook before going back to your caring responsibilities.

Family carers must look after their health. If you're feeling overwhelmed while caring for an elderly loved one, hire an experienced caregiver to offer senior home care. Families in Arlington who wish to avoid burnout might turn to Assisting Hands Home Care. While you snooze, go to work, conduct chores, or go on vacation, one of our experienced carers can help your loved one at home.

2. Participate in a movie marathon. Spend your break seeing the latest movies at the local cinema if you're a movie buff. You may make it a double or triple showcase with friends, or you can go alone to the cinema. Watching movies enables you to concentrate on something enjoyable rather than stressing about your loved one's present health state. Getting out of the home and having a movie night will momentarily soothe your thoughts and improve your mood.

3. Indulge in a spa retreat. Trips to the spa on a weekly or monthly basis might be enjoyable, but a spa vacation during a break from caring may offer you the most advantages. You might engage in activities that calm your mind and body, relieving stress and suffering while at the resort & spa. In a friendly setting, you may engage with like-minded individuals, unwind, and recharge. Instead of attending to your loved one, you may be pampered while engaging in enjoyable and relaxing activities.

You want to be an excellent caregiver for your loved one, therefore you must take care of yourself as well. Caring for elderly loved ones may be difficult for families who lack knowledge or practical qualifications in-home care, but you don't have to tackle this difficulty alone. Assisting Hands Home Care can provide the assistance that family carers need. We provide high-quality live-in and respite care, as well as Alzheimer's, dementia, stroke, and Parkinson's disease care.

4. Focus on goals.

Your goals before being a family caregiver shouldn't ever be abandoned. During your break, think about your objectives and what you can do to make them a reality. Spend your free time interacting with specialists who can help you achieve your objectives, no matter how long it takes. Working on your objectives keeps you from feeling regret, resentment, and other unpleasant feelings that caregivers often experience when they abandon their aspirations to care for their elderly parents.

5. Pick up a new skill.
After numerous days of putting your loved one's well-being ahead of your own, it's time to try something new, such as learning languages, taking a painting lesson, or joining an exercise class. Fun activities like these may keep you socially engaged while also providing you with a feeling of purpose. Move on to another interesting and exciting hobby during your next break after you've learned one new craft or activity. The process of learning crafts helps your creative abilities to flow, which may decrease stress,

lower blood pressure, and improve your overall quality of life.

Having a highly qualified caregiver join your caregiving team is another method to alleviate stress. A range of age-related health issues might make it more difficult for seniors to function freely.

www.ingramcontent.com/pod-product-compliance
Lightning Source LLC
Chambersburg PA
CBHW071927120726
48001CB00005B/1908